CREATE *Stunning*
Journals & Workbooks
Using *Canva*
& Createspace

Sarah Lentz

Dedication

I dedicate this book to the Designer of people (especially the fascinating and lovable people in my family – both immediate and extended)

Contents

Introduction

Here's what I hope you're thinking: "I'd like to design my own journal (or workbook). Maybe I'll even publish it and sell some copies. Maybe I'll go even further and make a series of beautiful and useful journals (or workbooks or planners) – and sell them on Amazon and other online booksellers."

You could totally do that, by the way. But where do you start?

Next, maybe you're thinking, "I don't know my way around Adobe Photoshop or InDesign, and I'm really not motivated to learn how to use them."

Or "it looks like it'll take forever, and I don't want to spend all my free time figuring it out. That's a lot of time that I'd rather spend writing (or doing other more important things)."

It could also be the price of using those programs – and wondering which one you'll really need to get the job done and done right.

Do you need Photoshop or InDesign? Or both? And, sure, there are video tutorials online to help you make sense of all the tools, but (if you're like me) one look at that interface makes you feel instant overwhelm, and you just want to scream, "WHY DOES IT HAVE TO BE SO COMPLICATED?!"

It doesn't. Because there's Canva.

Speaking from my own experience, from the beginning, I found Canva to be easier and more enjoyable to learn and easier to use – and a lot less overwhelming.

Not everyone is as easily overwhelmed as I am, but maybe you can relate.

Even after trying Adobe Photoshop's seven-day free trial period (which ended even when I bailed on the first day – after a few minutes – and then only opened it again after the seven days had passed, thinking (erroneously) that it would only count the days I was actually using it), I was no closer to feeling any inclination to sign up for a monthly membership.

I used the free version of Canva for months before I decided to try their Canva For Work (which I love). You don't even need the paid program, though, to create beautiful book covers - and have a ball doing so - with Canva.

I'm not just talking about ebook covers, though I've made those with Canva, too. Canva has a ready-made template for Kindle ebook covers, which I've used many times. I used it, in fact, to create the cover for this book.

In this book, though, we tackle something that many have assumed you can only create easily using Photoshop or InDesign.

A few months ago, I joined a journal design program that gave some ideas on how to create the whole cover using Canva, but it did involve some guesswork, and I wasn't comfortable just guessing at the width of the spine.

Fortunately, we don't have to.

Once we use a tool I'll show you in this book, you'll know the exact dimensions you need to use when creating your own custom-sized cover template – as well as for the individual parts of your cover (front, back, and spine).

From then, it's just a matter of designing those parts and snapping them into place using the step-by-step process described in this book.

You'll also have, at your disposal, links that will take you to invaluable resources for creating your journal covers.

Canva's tutorials can also be a big help (they have been for me), and you can also learn a lot by browsing book covers on Amazon and on cover design websites.

Then we'll move on to the interior of your journal - how to choose and download the Word template from the CreateSpace website and how to fill it with your own ideas, as well as any images, lines (for your customers to fill), quotes, charts, tables, etc.

When you're done reading this book, you'll know not only how to design and upload your own gorgeous journal and workbook covers, you'll know how to fill, prepare, and upload your journal or workbook interiors to CreateSpace and turn them into real paperback books.

When you order your first proof and hold it in your hands, you'll be glad you bought this book and created something you can be proud of. You can even order copies of them for friends and family.

If you like, you can make multiple covers for the same journal or workbook and publish them all on Amazon, with very little trouble and expense.

First, we'll design our cover – beginning with the parts and then putting them together.

Next, we'll tackle the interior, using a free, downloadable template from the CreateSpace website. Then, we'll upload both the interior and cover files (as PDFs) to CreateSpace for review.

We'll go over what happens between the review and publication, including how to order your own paperback proof and ensure that the journal will be available on the Amazon store for easy ordering.

I'm itching to get started, and I hope you are, too. Let's dig in!

1

Some words about design

Before you create your book's cover, it's worthwhile to touch on a few design basics. The title of this book does say "stunning," after all (not "decent" or "okay-looking"), and it makes sense to include some design tips that will help you create a cover you can be proud of.

Fonts / typefaces

In an article on SmashingMagazine.com ("'What Font Should I Use?' Five Principles for Choosing and Using Typefaces"), Dan Mayer gives us the following advice:

"Most of the time, one typeface will do, especially if it's one of our workhorses with many different weights that work together. If we reach a point where we want to add a second face to the mix, it's always good to observe this simple rule: 'keep it exactly the same, or change it a lot" – avoid wimpy, incremental variations.

"This is a general principle of design, and its official name is **correspondence and contrast**."

You've probably seen book covers with more than one typeface used, and many designers will tell you not to use more than three, and you've no doubt seen covers where three didn't feel like too many.

It depends on how they're used.

In some cases, two fonts can get your cover looking just the way you want it.

On the cover of my first book, three total fonts were used:

1. Dancing Script Bold for the words "The" and "Hypothyroid" and for the author name (in different sizes)

2. Lato in all caps for the word "Writer."

3. Josefin Sans for the subtitle

For my second book (this one), I use only two fonts: League Gothic and Dancing Script Bold.

For my third, so far, I have two – though I'm considering a third for the subtitle. Two feels simpler and cleaner to me, but some fonts work better for titles and others for subtitles (which are usually smaller).

As with colors, if you use too many fonts, the overwhelming effect can drown the message you want to convey. Keep it simple, and your message and the personality of each font will come through and have more impact.

Your journal or workbook may not need a subtitle, but if it does – and if the simpler (and more eye-friendly) of two fonts used in the title works well – that may be the one to go with.

Or if your title is all in a display font, you can choose a clean, serif or sans serif font for the subtitle.

Canva has some brief and helpful design tutorials mixing fonts and font variations. I've found them to be a big help.

If you want to use a font that Canva doesn't provide, Canva For Work allows you to add up to ten fonts. It's not free, but it's one of my bread-and-butter programs, so I'm keeping it.

You can find plenty of free fonts at the following sites (among others):

1. Google Fonts

2. Font Squirrel.com

3. FontSpace.com

4. MyFonts.com

5. FontRiver.com

While you can find scads of free fonts all over the web, don't rule out fonts you'd have to buy.

For one, Envato Market (at graphicriver.net) offers 2,186 fonts with prices starting at $3, and it can't hurt to look. You might find something with just the personality you want for the cover of your journal or workbook.

Colors

At TigerColor.com, they recommend a three color combination.

> "A three color combination is a good starting point. This is enough to create variation and visual interest. A triadic color scheme where the colors are equally spaced around the color circle is a good choice for beginners, because it is easy to get good results. The split complementary color scheme is another good alternative."

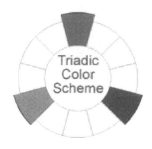

"Apply the 60 – 30 – 10 rule for success.

"You should not use equal amounts of the three colors. An old designer's rule is to divide the colors into percentages of 60, 30, and 10.

60%   10%   30%

"The **primary color** should cover about 60% of the space and create the overall unifying theme of the design. Then add about 30% of the **secondary color** to create contrast and visual interest. Finally use about 10% of the **accent color** to provide that final touch of elegance.

"A good example of this distribution of color is a man's business suit: 60% of the outfit is made up of the slacks and jacket. The shirt represents 30% and the tie, 10%."

For another take on color, Derek Murphy – writing for Joanna Penn's blog ("How to Make Your Own Free Book Cover in MS Word" on www.thecreativepenn.com) – gives us the following:

"You can use a color wheel to find complimentary colors (opposites / across from each other). Blockbuster movie posters usually use orange and teal (a lot of my book covers do also).

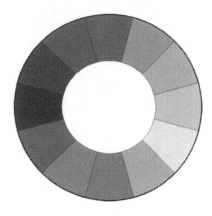

"Green and purple can work also.

"Unfortunately, Christmas ruined red and green, but red still goes well with black or white.

"Too many colors can be distracting, so try to go for one or two main colors (if the whole background is blue, you could use yellow text to stand out....)"

While there is no fixed answer on how many colors you should use for your cover, these should give you some ideas.

Layout

How your design elements are arranged can dramatically change the feel of a book cover.

Trying to squish too much text onto the cover, for instance – or too much of any design element – can make your cover look too busy or cluttered.

You don't want potential customers averting their eyes or reaching for their eye drops (or Xanax) after looking at the cover of your journal or workbook.

Your layout should show an appreciation for "white space," which is part of the overall picture and is responsible for part of the overall feel.

Think of a favorite room in your house. You need space to walk around the furniture. Every room is different, but no room should be so full of things that you can barely get around them. That isn't a room – it's a storage closet. Nobody wants to hang out in a storage closet (unless there's no alternative).

Arrange your words and other design elements in a way that they have some room to breathe and to show off a little – without being alienated from the other elements by *too* much space.

Canva's design tutorials on Layout include interactive lessons on "The Art of Alignment," "Working with White Space," and "Harnessing Hierarchy."

Canva design tutorials

Canva tutorials are free and great for getting acquainted with Canva's tools and learning some design tips (using color, mixing fonts, balancing design elements).

To access these, go to the Help menu tab on the top left side of the page for your project. Canva will open a new tab for their "Help Center," and you can roll your mouse pointer over the "Learn" tab at the top (right of center), which will bring up a menu that includes both "Design School" and "Tutorials," as well as "Teaching Materials" and "Design Courses."

I'd start with "Tutorials." I've learned a lot from them and haven't even gotten through them all. Canva provides a lot of helpful and user-friendly design guides for folks who don't have the time, money, or inclination to go to college and study graphic design.

Canva has tutorials for the following:

1. Advanced Tips

2. Backgrounds

3. Branding

4. Color

5. Fonts

6. Getting Started

7. Images

8. Layout

9. Shapes and Icons

10. Skills in Action

It's a low-stress, interactive way to learn the basics and to apply them. If you like playing with design and want to get better at it, you'll be glad you checked these out.

Canva design school

Canva also has some fantastic articles on their "Canva Design School" page that will help you beef up your design skills. I'll share a few here:

1. "Ten Tips to Teach Yourself Design and Boost Your Design Skills" by Sawaram

2. "50 Modern Fonts to Give Your Designs a Contemporary Feeling" by Rebecca Gross

3. "50 Free Futuristic Fonts to Help Make Your Designs Look Uniquely Alternative" by Maria Jose

4. "A simple trick we use at Canva to enhance our images and achieve brand consistency [with templates]" by Ritika Tiwari

5. "Ten Simple Ways to Enhance Your Images" by Janie Kliever

Create a book cover gallery

Sometimes, it's fun just to look at the book covers of best-selling books online, and it can be a great way to get ideas for your own covers.

Create a folder on your computer (titled "Book Cover Gallery" or whatever appeals to you) and save images of the book covers you like the best. You can group them by genre or by other criteria: the main/dominant color, the author (if you collect several from a specific author), or by a specific mood or flavor. Or you can simply separate the fiction covers from the nonfiction ones.

Have you ever looked at some covers and thought, "It takes a special kind of genius to design covers like these. How am I going to create something that won't look like crap compared to them?"

If you have zero experience designing book covers, don't expect your first finished book cover to be a work of art. The more covers you make – and subject to (constructive) criticism – the more you learn about what makes a book cover design great.

It'll never be perfect, though, so please don't keep your project in limbo until you can get the cover "just right." Just as with your book's interior, at some point, you just have to let go and send it off into the world – even if you have this nagging feeling that the cover could still be improved somehow.

Vulnerability and the budding book cover designer

Nobody is an expert designer right off the bat. We learn from others who've become experts (or who are at least further along than we are), and we keep learning as we create and take risks by exposing ourselves and our design babies to other people's opinions.

Just as writers must learn to expose their writing to the critical eye of an editor and then of their readers, anyone who designs a book cover that will be on display on Amazon's web pages must learn to risk criticism from others.

It can help to belong to a Facebook group where someone (ideally, the administrator) has real experience designing book covers and can provide knowledgeable and constructive criticism for those willing to post images of their book covers in the making.

There are groups for writers/authors on Facebook that will let you post an image of your book cover to receive constructive feedback from other group members. Otherwise, you can always post them on your personal Facebook page and ask your FB connections to let you know what they think of it.

You can also keep an eye out for covers you like on other authors' books and ask them who designed their covers. If that designer has a website you can visit, that's another place to get design ideas. If you decide, "Hey, I'd rather have this person design a cover for me," that's okay, too.

But otherwise, the more you collect cover designs for gallery and really think about why each cover appeals to you, the more you can bring to your own design table when you're working on your cover.

Create your own design portfolio

This can be a page on your blog or a separate blog (free or paid) from which you can share your images on social media, which can invite creative feedback from your social media contacts.

So far, my only portfolio is on my Canva page, under "All your designs," and I'm okay with that. But more and more I'm sharing my designs on my blog and on social media to get feedback, which I use to make them better.

The sooner you share your ideas for a cover design with others, the more you can create buzz about your new project and involve others in the process of making it better.

2

Creating the parts of your journal's / workbook's cover

Let's get started by opening Canva.

If you're completely new to Canva, you'll need to sign up for an account, which is free and quick to set up.

Once you've got that, we can get started by creating templates for the parts of your journal or workbook: the front cover, the back cover, and the spine.

Custom measurements

When it comes to your custom measurements, you'll need to keep in mind that with print books, the bleed area is about an eighth of an inch on all sides of the full cover and along the exterior edge of each page (or the front and back cover).

What is bleed, though?

"Bleed" is a printing term for the area around the edge of a page or cover that will be cut off. You'll want to keep that in mind if you have images that run to the outside edges of your page or text that's too close to the edge.

Usually, your text will be kept within the margins you set and shouldn't come anywhere near the bleed area, but if you have an image and don't want a particular feature trimmed off, you'll want to keep it well within the printed area rather than running off the edge. If a little trimming of your background image, pattern, or color won't affect the quality of your book project, then you have nothing to worry about.

But it does mean we need to add the bleed area to our custom dimensions.

So, if you want, say, a 6 by 9 inch book, you'll need to create a front and back cover piece that has those dimensions for width and height, with an eighth of an inch (0.125) added to width for the external edge (one of the edges), and with a quarter inch (0.25) added to height for the bleed at the top and bottom.

But what about the spine? How do we calculate that?

Here's where we open an extra browser tab for CreateSpace – specifically for the page devoted to creating and downloading a cover template (search for "cover template" on CreateSpace.com, and click on "Book Cover Template." It should take you to a page with the heading, "Book Help > Artwork & Templates.").

Those who prefer to use Photoshop can build on that template by adding layers, but we're going to use it just to calculate the width of your book's spine.

To do that, we need to know a few things:

1. The interior type (black & white or full color, with or without bleed)

2. Trim size (the size you want your book to be)

3. Number of pages

4. Paper color (white or cream)

If you don't know yet how many pages your journal or workbook will have, it helps to know how many days or sections you'll be creating pages for.

When I designed my journal, I decided I wanted to create eight pages for each of the thirty days covered by the journal. That adds up to 240 pages, but I also have my front and back pages:

1. Title page

2. Copyright page

3. The "this is what you get" or "how to use this journal" page

4. The dedication page

5. A snippet page (to jot down a one-line note for each of the thirty days)

6. A blank page before the 1st page of Day 1 (because I wanted the first page to land on an odd numbered page, so it would be on the right side).

7. The "Now that you've finished..." page at the end of the book.

That adds up to 247 pages. So, to create my template, I entered the following information

1. Interior type: Black & white (without bleed, because I don't need to see that on the template; I'm downloading it only for the spine width)

2. Trim size: 6" x 9"

3. Number of pages: 247

4. Page color: cream (because I like the look of cream paper better, but depending on the colors in your book's cover, you may want to go with white)

Then I click on "Build template," and CreateSpace gives me a zip file to download – which contains the template in two different formats: PNG and PDF. I'm more interested in the PDF, though the template looks the same in either format.

After downloading, I'll click on the PDF and open it to find that my spine width is 0.63 inches.

And I'll save it to my desktop or to a folder I created for my book – for future reference.

But this is how easy it is to find our spine measurement, and when it's time to create our book's spine in Canva, now we know the measurement to enter into the width field.

Bonus: the template also shows where CreateSpace will put the barcode and ISBN numbers. CreateSpace will assign your book an ISBN number – if you ask them to – when you're creating it on their website.

We're ready to go!

Making your front and back covers

First of all, to begin with the front cover, click on "Create a Design" on the left-hand side of your Canva screen and then go to the top right to "Use Custom Dimensions" and click on that.

(You could also bypass the "Create a Design" and go right to the "Use Custom Dimensions" button on the top right).

First, change the unit to inches (in), rather than pixels (px), and then enter your dimensions for width and height, including bleed (adding 0.125 to width and 0.25 to height).

So, for a 6 x 9 inch book, we'd enter 6.125 inches (width) and 9.25 inches (height).

Then click on "Design."

To the right of your custom-sized front cover template, you'll see a number 1 and an icon that looks like one page resting on the bottom right corner of another. Click on that to create a duplicate copy of your front cover template, and now you have the foundations of both your front and back covers.

You can use this icon to create duplicates in order to play with different text arrangements while keeping the same background, to create different cover options to choose from.

Canva will allow you to create up to 30 pages for each design file, but that gives you plenty of pages to work with. If 30 isn't enough, you can always create a new design, give it the same dimensions, and have up to 30 more templates (pages) to play with.

Check the left side of the Canva screen. Canva should have the tab for "layouts" open for you, but we don't need that one just yet. We'll use one of those layouts for the whole cover template.

For now, check out the other tabs and get acquainted with some of Canva's offerings (especially the "Elements": free photos, grids, frames, shapes, lines, illustrations, icons, charts, and "I♥Canva.").

Check out the free photos (under the "Elements" tab) – as well as those that aren't free. You might find something you'd like to add to your journal cover.

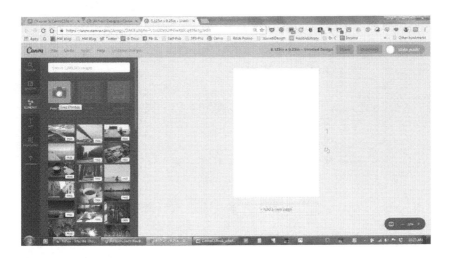

If you like one of the $1 images, Canva will let you play with a watermarked version (with a lattice overlay and the word Canva in faded letters across the front) until you want to download a copy, at which point it'll ask you to pay $1 for 24-hours' worth of use.

I've done this and just gone to town downloading thirty or more different versions of the same cover within that 24-hour period to make the most of my access to that image (without the watermark) – trying different fonts, different arrangements, etc. It's one of the least expensive options for paid images, and you can use the search field to focus your options.

Images from outside sources

If you don't find an image here that makes you think, "That could work!" there are a number of online sources of royalty-free images. Some are free, and some are not.

I like to browse the free ones first, usually, and then check the paid ones if I can't find anything I like on the free sites. For this book's cover, I used an image from Shutterstock.

Free royalty-free images:

1. Pixabay.com

2. PhotoPin.com

3. OpenClipArt.org

4. Unsplash.com

5. Freedigitalphotos.net

6. FreeImages.com

7. The free section of DreamsTime.com

Royalty-free images for a price (that varies from one provider to the next). The good news with these is you can download a water-marked version of the image and try it out with Canva to see if it's the right image for your cover – before you buy it (at which point they let you download a copy of the image without the watermark).

1. iStockPhotos.com

2. ShutterStock.com

3. Fotolia.com (by Adobe)

4. BigStock.com

5. DreamsTime.com

Text

Add your title, subtitle, and author name using the text feature. This is one feature that is upgraded for the paid version of Canva (Canva For Work), and I'll go into that in the bonus chapter at the end of this book, if you'd like to know more about why I decided to pay for it. But for this project, the free version – and all its features – will do just fine.

Canva has, by default, certain fonts picked out for heading-size text, subheading-size text, and body text, but once you click on one of the text options, you can edit the font and font-size, as well as the color and other features.

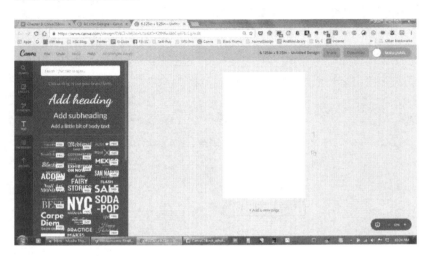

If you're near-sighted like me, go ahead and start with the "Add heading" text option and enter something, even if it's just your name – or your book's title, if you already have one. Up at the top of your editing window, you'll see the editing bar, with the font name at the far left. You can go ahead and click on that to change it to another font you like.

Editing tools
The font-size is right next to that, so you can make your first text feature larger or smaller. You can even, while the number is highlighted, enter your own value for the text size, which is crucial, because the sizes offered on the drop-down menu may not have just the right font-size for a particular bit of text.

You can do this with Word, too, but I only found out after months with Canva that I could enter my own custom font size. I hadn't needed to, before, so I hadn't tried.

When you roll your cursor over your text, you'll notice that around the edges of your text box, the pointer will change to a four-directional pointer, which is your **positioning tool**. Hold down your left mouse button and drag to position the text just where you want it on your template.

The **rotation tool** is there if you want to set any of your text at an angle or turn it completely 90 degrees – which we'll need to do to position it correctly for your book's spine.

You can change the text alignment to center, left justify, or right justify the text in a particular text box. You can use the **uppercase/lowercase toggle** icon to switch your text from its current mix of upper and lower case letters to full uppercase and back again.

You can also add a **bulleted list** – which I love for listing the benefits of your book on the back cover, as well as for a front-matter page that lists the features of your journal or workbook.

Text spacing allows you to change the spacing between the letters or the spacing between lines of text in your text box. Playing with text spacing can give your text arrangements are more eye-catching and professional look.

And the ability to adjust **line spacing** is invaluable when you want to fit more lines of text in a tight space, without making it look too cramped (which depends on your choice of font and font-size).

Further over to the right on your editing bar, you'll see **"Copy,"** which lets you make an identical copy of something you've selected on your template – whether it's text, an image, or another feature from the

Canva toolbox. I use this often to duplicate my text box when I want to retain that particular font but change the text.

If you'll notice, while you're dragging things across your template, you'll see guidelines pop up at the center to let you know that your selection is centered. You'll also see a horizontal guideline when you reach the horizontal middle. Both guidelines will show up when you're exactly at the center.

Also, when you're positioning text or other large enough features, you'll see guidelines that stretch from other features to let you know when the item you're dragging is in alignment with it. I appreciate this when I'm trying to line one bit of text up with text from another text box.

Why would you have separate text boxes, anyway? With Canva, you can only have one font and one font size per text box. You can have different colors for different words or letters in the same text box, but for some reason, if you want to change the font for a selected bit of text, it'll change the font for all the text in that box.

Trade-offs. No program is perfect, but it's easy with Canva to use the copy feature and make as many text boxes as we need. The plus side? It allows us to position our bits of text just the way we want them on the cover.

The **"Arrange"** feature is probably faded right now, unless you already have something behind your text, such as a background picture or a feature from Canva's "Elements." Arrange allows us to either push our selected item to the back (behind the item it's currently blocking) or bring it up front). Usually, when we're selecting something to "Arrange," we're pushing it "back" to bring hidden text to the front.

Next is the **transparency** feature, which you'll see as an icon that looks a tiny checkerboard that's fading on the right side. Click on that and drag the circle along the Transparency scale to make it fade or come in more clearly. By default, it's at full-pigment.

Next, you'll see a **paperclip** icon, which allows you to insert a hyperlink – which can be useful if you're creating a downloadable list of resources, and you want the recipients of that list to be able to easily access the resources by simply clicking on the links.

Last is the tiny trash can, which allows you to delete whatever item you've selected. If you delete something by accident, you can go to Canva's upper left-hand menu and hit the "Undo" button.

You can even browse and select one of Canva's stylized text arrangements – below the three main text-adding options (heading, subheading, and body text) and simply change the words to your own. You can change the colors of these arrangements, too, as well as the fonts and font-sizes.

Click and drag the corners or use the repositioning tool to get the text or arrangement where you want it – and get each element to the size you want for your cover.

The **"BkGround"** tab is another source of images and textures you can add to your cover. I'm partial to using images, as long as I can make them work with my title and (if I have one) subtitle, but I've used a simple background color for one of my journals, and if you want to go that route, you can have more room to work with for your text arrangement.

Another option is to use a background image but also superimpose a shape for a text-box and use the "Transparency" feature (while editing your text-box shape) to fade it out and allow the background to show through -- but without obscuring the text (which you can bring up front by clicking on "back" to shove the shape to the back, as many times as necessary to bring other elements (anything hidden by the shape) to the front.

The back cover

If you're not sure what to put on your book's back cover, a good bet is to take your book description (after you've written one), keeping it to 300 words or fewer, and use that.

You can also add a small author portrait on the bottom left side and even a brief author bio, making sure to avoid the area reserved for the book's ISBN numbers and bar code.

Here's a screenshot of my journal's back cover in Canva. I didn't bother with an author photo, but I did add the url for my blog at the bottom left.

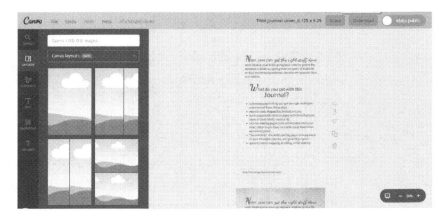

I used the same fonts and colors and dressed up the first letter of each paragraph.

Your back cover should be as pleasing to the eye as the front, though the front is what usually leads people to check out your back cover.

Both are important. A badly-designed back cover can detract from an otherwise attractive journal or workbook.

Saving & downloading

Once you've gotten your front cover and back cover looking the way you want them to (with the right background, images, and text), save your work and download your images using the button at the top right of your screen.

It'll give you some options, and for now we want either the JPG or the PNG format for these parts. When you download multiple images (pages), Canva will download it as a zip file, but when you open it, you'll have the chance to click on each individual image file, and open it using one of the photo editing programs on your PC (like Windows Paint for PNG files).

My favorite photo editing tool is a free downloadable editor called PhotoScape, which allows me to edit JPG files and then save them to my desktop (or anywhere else on my computer, but saving them to my desktop makes it easier to find when I want to upload them back into Canva for the full cover template).

Paint.net is another free and useful photo-editing program. I like the feel of it better than Gimp, which is a free program that can be used to edit Photoshop files. As a Photoshop flunkie, I don't have much use for Gimp.

Now, for your spine

Custom-make another template with your spine width and with same length measurement (including bleed) you used for your front and back covers.

27

Give it the same background or one that will complement the front and back cover pieces. Then add some text and use the rotational tool to position it correctly on the spine (so when you crane your neck to your right, you can read the text).

Make sure the type is small enough not to get too close to the edges of your spine. You want it to be large enough to read but small enough to comfortably fit on the spine with some white space on either side of it.

Position the title about an inch from the top of the spine, and place your name (full or last) an inch from the bottom. If your name won't fit on the spine with your title, you can make it smaller or just leave it off. With journals & workbooks, your author name doesn't need to be on the spine, though I like to put my last name on mine, if it'll fit.

Save and download – again as a JPG or a PNG, whichever is easiest for you to edit (if you need to) – and save to your desktop or to a dedicated folder on your desktop.

In the next chapter, we'll create a full cover template and prepare it for the parts you just made. Then, we'll put it all together and download it. And you'll be that much closer to having your journal / workbook / planner ready to upload to CreateSpace.

The second chapter is a short one (comparatively), so if you've got your cover parts ready, you're closer to having a full cover created than you might think.

Can't wait to get it done? Let's head on over to Chapter 3, then.

3

Creating the full cover template & assembling the whole

N ow, it's time to create your full cover template and prepare it for the 3 parts you just made.

Click on "Use custom dimensions" (or "Create a Design" and then "Use custom dimensions") and change the unit from px (pixels) to in (inches).

For width, you'll want to add the width dimensions of all the pieces you just made.

So, for my 6 x 9 inch book, I added 6.125 (front cover width) to 6.125 (back cover width) to 0.63 (spin width) to get a total width of 12.88.

For the height, all we need is the same height measurement we used for all three pieces. We're not stacking our cover pieces vertically, so the height remains the same.

The magic is in the layout

Next, you'll look over on the left side of the Canva design screen -- particularly at the layouts -- and you'll select the one that cuts the page in half vertically.

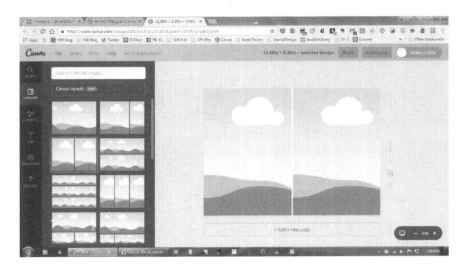

It looks like a two-pane window or an open book with an identical scene on both pages. On my page, it's the second layout down on the left of two columns. In the screenshot above, you can see it outlined in blue.

Once you click on that layout, it will cover your template (as you can see in my screenshot above), and you can now begin uploading your cover parts and positioning them.

Uploading & assembly

Click on "Uploads" and then "Upload your own images" to find your front cover, your back cover, and your spine.

Once you upload them to your Canva image library, you can click on them one at a time to add them to your cover template & position them.

You'll notice that when you drag the front cover over the right hand pane of the Canva split-pane layout, Canva will want to put your front cover right inside that pane (whereas if you position it over the center, it'll just drop the cover piece right front and center on the layout). Let it. Canva will want to put it in one pane or the other, so make sure you're positioning it over the right pane before you let go.

The front cover fits in the right-hand pane, and the back cover fits in the left-hand pane.

Once you click on the spine, it will go to the tiny gap between the two panes. It needs only to be gently stretched at the top and bottom until the dotted line at the top (and then the bottom) meets a dotted line (that will appear when the edges meet) for the whole template.

Then, you'll save the whole cover and download it to your desktop as a JPG or PNG and then, when you've got it looking just the way you want it to look for your journal or workbook, you'll download it as a print PDF and save that to your desktop (or dedicated folder) for uploading to CreateSpace.

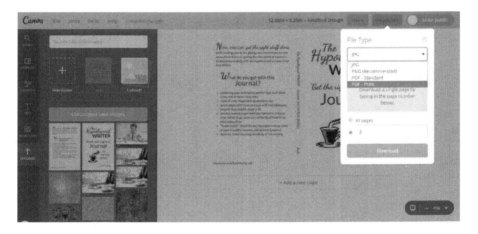

Critical Note: When NOT to use the layout

If your book's spine isn't big enough to support text – and CreateSpace's website gives us a guideline for this (fewer than 110 pages means no text on the spine, and there may not be much of a spine to speak of) – you'll want to avoid using a layout with your full cover template.

If your book isn't big enough to support a spine with text, create a custom-sized full cover template using the spine width calculated by CreateSpace (on your downloaded cover template), added to the width of your front and back cover pieces.

Then, simply position your front and back covers along the right-most and left-most edges (respectively) of your full cover template and fill in the background with a color that matches your cover.

You'll notice when you upload and click on your front and back cover pieces to add them to your template that they won't be the same size they were before (if they were, they'd be just as tall as your template).

So, what you'll need to do – since you don't have a layout that automatically resizes your front and back pieces to fit them into the panes – is drag the front piece over the right side, until it's flush with the edge (you'll see the dotted lines appear when the edge of your piece meets the edge of your template), and then, if it's not also flush with the top edge, drag the top left corner to make the top edge of the cover piece meet the top edge of the template, and do the same with the bottom, using the guideline that appears at the bottom edge of the template when the edges meet.

You can see what I mean from the screenshot below. When you're done positioning both the front and back cover pieces, you'll have a white strip between them which will need to be filled with something (unless a white strip looks fine with your cover, and you'd like to keep it that way).

I went back and found the hex code for the color I used for the front and back pieces and copied it.

I added the code by clicking on the plus box under "Document colors" and pasting my copied hex code into the field, replacing the code that was already there.

Then, once my background color was one of the "Document colors," I clicked on the white space between my cover pieces and then clicked on one of the default background colors available and then clicked on my background color.

For some reason, Canva won't let me just click right from the space I need to color to one of the "Document colors," but if I select a background color or pattern and *then* click on a document color, it works fine.

You can also begin with the same image or pattern overlay that you used for your front and back pieces and then position your front and back cover pieces, leaving that center sliver open.

Making changes

You have a finished book cover!

But is it the final version? Not necessarily.

You can make as many changes to it as you like before you download it as a PDF and upload it to CreateSpace. Give yourself some time to play with it and look up covers you like on Amazon or the websites of book cover designers to get more ideas.

The more you do this, the better you'll get at designing a cover that you love. If this first one doesn't knock your socks off, there are some things you can do to make it better.

1. Post a few different cover images on Facebook and ask people to vote on their favorite and to tell you why they liked it or what they might suggest to make it better.

2. Find someone on Fiverr.com who designs covers for $5 and ask them to design a cover for you. Even if you don't like it, you're only out $5, and you might at least get some ideas on how to make your cover better.

3. Cruise the image sites for pics that you love, and just keep playing with different cover ideas until you settle on the one you like best for your first journal (or workbook or planner).

4. Look over your own book collection and ask yourself what you like about your favorite book covers among them. Pick one and ask what about the cover appeals to you? The colors? The images or how they

and the words of the title and subtitle are arranged? The different text sizes and fonts and how the designer managed to unify all the elements?

Go back to your cover and see if there's anything you could change on the front or back cover that would make it look more appealing to you. You can always redo the parts, download them again, and upload them to snap into place on your full cover template.

5. Look over some Canva tutorials for design ideas and apply what you learn.

In the next chapter, we'll download an interior template from the CreateSpace website (using a link I've provided) and begin filling it for your journal or workbook.

4

CreateSpace interior templates

Before you download your interior template from CreateSpace, you need to know what size you want for your book – which is called the "trim size."

If you've already designed your cover, though, you already know what size you need.

Once you've clicked on the CreateSpace link, you should see a chart with trim sizes and two options for downloadable templates: basic and formatted.

The formatted templates include sample formatted content which you can replace with your own.

I used the simple template for my first journal, and I'm using a formatted template for my next paperback book – just to get a sense of which one I prefer. If you know exactly what to put in the front matter and back matter pages (title page, copyright page, dedication page, introduction, about the author page, etc.), the basic template will do just fine.

If you want to see where everything goes (and it can't hurt to be reminded sometimes), go with the formatted template.

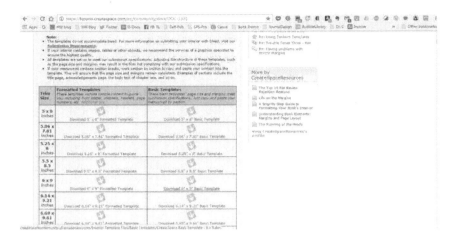

Preparing the template

There are a few things we should do to prepare your template for the main body of your journal or workbook (or planner).

1. Add page numbering, if you want it. In Word, this is in the "Insert" menu in the "Header & Footer" section.

2. Add headers and/or footers, if you want them (same place as page numbering)

3. Choose your fonts

4. Add the front matter

5. Add the back matter

Choose your fonts for the following:

1. title

2. headings (at the top of the page to announce new chapters, sections, activities, etc.)

3. subheadings (breaking up the chapter, section, etc. into smaller chunks)

4. normal text (everything but the fancy stuff)

As long as you embed your fonts before saving your completed interior file as a PDF and uploading it to CreateSpace, you can revel in the fact that print books don't limit you nearly as much as ebooks when it comes to font styles.

If you have any trademark fonts you like to use, enjoy using them. Keep in mind, though, that you want to keep it easy on your reader's eyes. As great as that cursive font looks for large headings, it's brutal at 12 point.

Shawn, the CreateSpace Graphic Arts Specialist, recommends a serif font (like Times New Roman) for interiors and particularly body text (normal text, as Word calls it) and a sans serif font for display text – which would include titles, headings, and subheadings, and other bits of text that are meant to draw attention to themselves.

Here's that list of free font sources online (so you won't have to jump back to Chapter 1).

1. Google Fonts

2. Font Squirrel.com

3. FontSpace.com

4. MyFonts.com

5. FontRiver.com

Black & white versus full color

The only thing that can make your book more expensive to produce is color. I'm not saying you can't include full color images, but printing the interior in full color is much more expensive than printing it in black and white.

Check out the "Member Order Calculator" on the CreateSpace Products page (createspace.com/products/book). You'll find it under the "Buying Copies" tab, and you can then enter your values for interior type (black & white or full color, with or without bleed), trim size, number of pages (put something in, even if you haven't nailed this down, yet), and number of copies. Click on calculate, and it'll tell you the cost per copy and the total cost (based on the quantity).

A 6" by 9" book with 247 pages, printed in black & white (excluding the cover, of course) costs $3.82 per copy

A 6" by 9" book with 247 pages, printed in full color costs $18.21 per copy

So, the cost difference is pretty hefty. Unless you really need color on the interior pages, I'd stick with black and white. Not many people are willing to pay that much extra just to have full color images inside their journals, workbooks, and planners.

Your cover, of course, will be printed in full color.

Front matter

Go ahead and skip this part (and the back matter section, too, if you like), if you already know what you intend to add to your book's 'before and after" pages.

If you're not 100% certain what to add, here are some possibilities, though not all are necessary, and you may find yourself creating new before and after pages that add even more value to your journal or workbook.

Front matter pages:

1. title page

2. copyright page

3. dedication page (optional)

4. acknowledgments page (optional)

5. preface (optional)

6. table of contents (optional)

7. Introduction (optional)

8. a "How to use this journal / workbook / planner" page

Back matter:

1. the "Now that you've finished…" page

2. the "about the author" page (include a list of your other books, your blog or website, and/or social media profiles, and show your customers how they can reach you with questions and suggestions).

3. a list of helpful resources (books, websites, courses, Etsy storefronts, etc.)

The Resource list at the back of this book has some articles that you may find helpful when designing your book. I've hyperlinked them to make it easier to access them.

It was while I was working on my journal that I decided to use one of my front matter pages as a "snippet page," with numbered lines (1 through 30), so that users could jot down a little something for each of the 30 days covered by the journal.

I say this, because you may get some brilliant ideas while you're working on your interior pages – or while you're taking a break (running an errand, taking a shower, doing chores around the house, etc.) – and someday you may even find yourself writing a book about all the ideas you came up with.

Whatever it leads to, I hope you enjoy creating your journal or workbook, and I'm honored that you're reading this book.

CreateSpace formatting requirements

CreateSpace interior templates do not include bleed, nor do they account for the fact that a book with three hundred pages will need larger interior margins (the gutter, which is where the pages are bound together to the spine) than a book with 200 or fewer pages.

CreateSpace provides a chart on their website and in their free PDF *Submission Specification* – with margin recommendations based on page count. To check it out, go to CreateSpace.com, search for "Submission specifications," and click on "Book Interior Guidelines." You should land on a page with the heading, "How to Create an Interior PDF of Your Book."

With my first journal, I noticed that the numbered lists – the ones with the numbers on an outside margin – were losing their numbers. So, I edited the interior file and gave the whole thing a slightly larger outside margin, which corrected the problem.

All I did was select all the file's contents with Ctrl-A, and then, using the ruler at the top of the page (below the file menus), I budged the marker for the left margin over just one tick to the right.

You can do the same on the right-side pages with the right margin marker. Since numbers on right-hand pages were on the inside margin – and were fine – I didn't change the outside margin, since I didn't see any problems with it.

A quicker way to change the outside margin, of course, is to go into Page setup, and change the outside margin from there, which will change it for both left-hand and right-hand pages.

One thing I love about CreateSpace, though, is the ease of changing your book even after it's published – just by uploading a new cover or a new interior file.

You *will* have to resubmit the whole book for review after changing either the cover or the interior file, and then, after CreateSpace accepts your files, you'll then have to preview and accept them for publication, but this takes a few days at the most.

In the next chapter, we'll fill the pages of your book with some basic journal and workbook features, and I'll share some ideas on how to make your first journal or workbook something your users will want to buy again and again.

These books are meant to be filled – and hopefully saved. We want to make them as easy and enjoyable to fill as possible.

See you in the next chapter!

5

Creating your journal / workbook interior

Listing your book's elements

I like to make a list of what I want to include in a particular journal or workbook, and it's easier to take it by sections – or days – and really think about what I'd like a journal of my own to include.

I'll give you some examples of pages I've put in my own published journals.

1. lined pages (some with writing prompts at the top, which are usually simple and designed to invite users to write whatever is on their minds)

2. blank pages (for mind-mapping, list-making, or sketching)

3. pages with lines and blank space (for a combination of drawing and writing)

4. quote pages (a quote at the top with lines beneath for the user to respond to it or to a quote-related prompt)

5. idea list pages "ten ideas for _____" (including some that are proof you told your inner editor to take a nap while you let the ideas flow)

6. a planning page for the user to write down the one most important thing to accomplish that day, plus three other important tasks.

7. a checklist so the user can check off certain tasks or habits after performing them that day – and an accompanying log page to jot down notes about each task or habit.

Put yourself in your reader's/customer's place and ask yourself what you would want to see in a journal or workbook of the type you want to create.

The purpose of your book will help with this. Is it more important to you that those who buy your books have plenty of room to record their own thoughts and ideas? Do you want to guide their thinking with questions, quotes, poetry, religious texts, or lessons learned by those who've accomplished what your book's buyers hope to accomplish?

What benefits do you want your customers to get from your journal or workbook (or planner)?

Possible benefits:
1. Unburden your mind of its thoughts and sort them out

2. Get more important things done

3. Stress less & accomplish more

4. Pray more or pray with more focus or more gratitude

5. Generate more ideas for various writing projects & keep a record of them

6. Record new ideas and develop each one with questions, lists, etc.

7. Master the concepts learned in a book, course, or training program

8. Choose a goal and work toward it steadily with daily objectives

9. Identify a project (book, novel, collection of short stories, etc.) and work toward its completion with daily, realistic, and measurable objectives

10. Begin and stick with a daily exercise program and log daily progress and weekly/monthly results

And there are plenty more. You may have thought of some as you read the list. Take some time to brainstorm a list of ideas (writing them down, of course – possibly in an idea journal of your own).

Once you know the answer to that question, you have a much better idea of what to write for your book's description – which will show up not only in the CreateSpace store but also on the book's Amazon sales page.

And once you know how many pages you'll need for each day of your journal or each lesson or section of your workbook, you'll have a much better idea of how many total pages your finished book will have.

Which will enable you to calculate – if you haven't already – a more accurate spine width for your book's cover.

And, fortunately, if the spine width for your cover isn't what it should be, it's easy to remake your cover with the correct spine measurement – even if you can't use the "Change Dimensions" option (which is only available in Canva For Work).

Creating a new cover template with the correct measurements, adding the layout, and then dropping in the front and back cover pieces takes only seconds.

Creating a new spine with the correct spine width and then adding the text takes a little longer – but not much.

Then, adding it to the cover template and downloading the whole as a PDF doesn't take long, either. Canva makes it quick and easy even when you're working with the free version.

Knowing the page count but not the content

When I designed my first journal, I decided I wanted the completed journal to be around 240 pages, and since I wanted the journal to cover "the first 30 days," it made sense to allot eight pages per day.

What I didn't know at the outset was how I was going to fill those eight pages.

So, I made a list of all the possible uses for those pages, and then I narrowed it down to my favorites.

And then, once I had that sorted, I went to work designing each type of page, deciding on fonts and font sizes and deciding which pages should be on the left-hand side and which on the right.

I wanted the checklist and the log page to face each other, since they both had to do with practicing the seven habits described in my book.

And I wanted the first of the eight pages to be the planning page, where users would identify the one thing they most wanted to get done that day — and three other things they wanted to accomplish besides.

After the pages were set up for the first day, I selected and copied the eight pages and pasted them over and over and over again, until I had thirty days' worth.

And then it was time to add the content:

1. quotes and related questions or prompts

2. prompts for the free-writing pages (2 pages of mostly lines)

3. list-making prompts (particularly the part that comes after the words "ten ideas for ____ (including some that will...")". The idea was to encourage my journal users to give themselves permission to write down even ridiculous ideas, just to send their inner editors running away with their ears covered — so they could get those ideas out of their heads and get in the habit of ditching the filter when it's time to make a list of ideas.

Also, by the end of 30 days, my journal users would have recorded 300 ideas. And some of those are bound to be useful for future projects.

Embellishments (curlicues, clip art, etc.)

Now come the adornments that you can easily add to your journal or workbook to dress up the interior and make it more pleasing to the eye — even if it's still in black and white.

Using the clip art in Word

In the Insert Menu, you'll find "Clip Art" in the Illustrations section, between "Picture" and "Shapes."

Click on it, and a side panel will open on the right with a search field and a filter to narrow down your search. Looking up the word "Journal" brings up quite a few options, many of which are in color. While that doesn't preclude you from using them if you're planning to have your book printed in black and white, you will have to keep that in mind and try to choose something that will look good even if the colors are changed to shades of gray.

Also, you'll notice that while that clip art panel is open, typing quickly becomes difficult. The panel seems to slow down the computer's responsiveness to your keyboard – at least that's what I noticed. I had to type much more slowly, or not all my letters showed up.

Closing the clipart panel cleared that up, but I'm adding this in case you experience the same frustrating lag time with your keyboard – at least if you're trying to type while keeping the clip art panel open.

In Word, we can't grab hold of the clipart image and position it exactly where we want – as we can in Canva. If you're wanting to create an ebook version, you'll want to avoid using tabs to position anything.

Probably the best bet is to stick the clip art at either the left end or the right end of headings or to center them as markers between sections of text.

Case in point:

Clip art on the outside

At the bottom of your clip art panel, you'll see a link to "Find more at Office.com," which takes you to a page with the headline, "Add online pictures or clip art to your file." From here, using the step-by-step instructions provided, you can do an image search on Bing and filter your results by clicking on the "License" menu and selecting "Free to modify, share, and use commercially."

If you want to narrow your search to clip art, just add "clip art" to your search term.

Click on something you like to see a full size image, and if you want it for your book, right click and "save image as" (or "save picture as," depending on your browser), and save it to your desktop or to a dedicated folder, where you can easily retrieve it using the "Insert" function in Word.

Word will even let you add a frame to pretty up your image, if you like. Double-click on your image to bring up the "Picture Tools."

Another source of free clipart is at OpenClipArt.org. You can easily search for the type of image you want, download it and save it to your desktop, and then upload it using the "Insert" function in Word. Below is an image from this site, saved as a .bmp file.

A word about image types
When you find an image on OpenClipArt.org and want to download it, keep in mind that if you simply hit the "download" button, the image will download as a .svg file, which Word does not like (for some reason). I tried repeatedly to save it to my desktop and then grab it with the Insert function, but Word didn't even recognize it.

So, I went back to the image's page and looked at my file type options, which include small, medium, and big PNG files, a PDF file, and one for Microsoft Office / LibreOffice, which is in WMF format. Oddly enough, when I clicked on the downloaded file, it opened in Windows Paint and saved as a .bmp file – which Word likes just fine.

Sometimes, though, I'll select the "Microsoft Office/LibreOffice" image option, and the image will get murdered in transit (no idea why), so I'll download one of the .PNG files instead, open it with  either Paint.net or Microsoft Office to save it as a .PNG file to my desktop, and then insert it from there.

Also, if there's a chance you'll want to convert your book to ebook format – though Amazon won't let you turn a basic journal (mostly lines) into an ebook – avoid doing a copy and paste with images. Kindle doesn't like it. CreateSpace is fine with it, though.

Since I'm creating this book for Kindle, I'm sticking with the "Insert" function. I'd rather not have to go through the book and replace all my copied-and-pasted images with inserted ones.

Lines

When I first created the interior file for my book in Canva, all I did to create lines for my journal was to hold down Shift and the dash/under-slash key to create an extended under-slash, which works just fine.

And you can do the same in Word.

_____

You can either hold it down until you've got several lines worth of under-slashes that just run from one line to the next, or you can create a line of a particular length and then copy and paste it over and over again until you have as many lines as you need.

_____

_____

_____

I've centered my lines, but there's nothing wrong with left-justifying or even right-justifying yours, if you prefer them that way.

You can even add an image and create lines that wrap around it in a certain way.

_____

_____

_____

_____

To do this, right-click on your image once you insert it onto the page, select "Wrap text," and then the option that you want. I chose "Tight" for this, but I also liked "Square."

Then, I simply added a line, made it as long as I wanted it, copied it, hit enter and then Ctrl-V to paste it, then enter and Ctrl-V another couple times to make a total of four lines.

(Note: This works a lot better for paperback books than for ebooks, because Kindle will take my image and shrink it. Experienced Kindle formatters may know a way around this, but for CreateSpace, we don't really have to worry about it).

You can also create your own image on Canva, save it as a .PNG file, insert it onto the page, and use it as a visual writing prompt for the lines you add beside it.

Text boxes

You can also add a text box, using the "Insert" menu and selecting "Text box" from the "Text" menu section on the far right – just to the left of "Symbols."

Just keep in mind that, by default, the text box will cover the text already on your page. If you select and then right-click on your text box, you can change the way it behaves toward surrounding text.

Again, you can choose "Wrap text" and change the arrangement until you like what you see. I chose "In line with text" this time, mostly because the neat arrangement I had with "Square" went all wonky on me once I saved the book as a filtered web page and then opened it with Kindle Previewer.

These look better in Word and PDF than in mobi format – which (as you can see) reduces your text box to a thumbnail image that you can (at least in Kindle Previewer) click on to enlarge it. Otherwise, reading it on your Kindle will be a challenge.

Again, though – not an issue with CreateSpace and paperback books.

A Note about copying and pasting text into your interior file

Don't do it. At least don't copy and paste text from a different program.

I had a head against the table moment when I realized why some of my text and lines came back shaded in my journal. When I realized why, it was a little embarrassing, and, to be honest, I'm still working on redoing my interior file to get rid of the shading — because the pages without it look better.

So, learn from my mistake, and don't copy your text from somewhere else (say, interior pages created on Canva, for a totally random example) and paste it into your Word document for your book — unless you like the shaded look. It's a personal choice.

Check out my journal on Amazon (for a limited time) if you want a peek at the shaded look. You can see it just by searching for and selecting *The Hypothyroid Writer* Journal and clicking on the cover to get a preview of the first few pages. It'll take me some time to get that redone and to update the book file on CreateSpace, and it'll take another day or three for Amazon to post the less shady, updated version.

You can totally copy and paste text from one Word document to another or from one place in your Word document to somewhere else. But if you're wanting to copy and paste text from another program — whether it's Canva, Google Docs, or Scrivener — I can tell you from my experience that copying and pasting from Canva will make your text print with shading. As for the other two — or other programs — I'd pay close attention when uploading your interior file — to how they look on CreateSpace's Interior Previewer. If they look shady, and you'd rather they didn't, you'll have to redo your interior without copying and pasting from those programs.

It may help, though, to copy and paste the content to a text file, first, and then to your Word doc — stripping it of any subversive formatting elements from its previous home. Think of it as giving a new dog a flea dip and all its shots before letting it into your home to play with your kids. It's a tiny bit like that.

I'm totally going to try that, by the way. Or I'll just recreate the first day's eight pages and then copy and paste them twenty-nine times. Then, I'll have to change the stuff that changes day by day (which is what will take a while; I really went all out to make this journal as entertaining as it is useful).

On second thought, I'll just recreate the shady parts and insert them onto the pages that need them – around the day-specific content I still have (which shouldn't be shaded, since I added it afterward). I can still copy and paste, but one feature at a time (most of those features being groups of so many lines, as well as my checklist and log pages). That'll be quicker.

I'm sharing my process with you, because you may find yourself having to redo things, and I like to at least try to use my mistakes for good. I make so many of them, after all. Might as well share the wealth.

Embedding the fonts

Before you save your file as a PDF (before uploading it to CreateSpace), you'll need to embed your fonts. To do this, go into the "File menu," and select "Options." From there, you'll choose "Save" and go to the bottom of the window to check "Embed fonts in the file" and leave the following two conditions unchecked.

Then click "OK" at the bottom right of the page, and you're set.

Saving your interior file as a PDF

Go to "Save as" in the file menu, and under "Save as type" (below the file name field), open the drop-down menu, and choose PDF (*.pdf).

Save in a location that will be easy for you to remember and to access when you're ready to upload the file to CreateSpace.

In the next chapter, we'll put everything together on CreateSpace and submit it for review. If you're all set, let's get right into it!

6

Putting it all together with CreateSpace & submitting your files for review

Now that you've got both your cover file and your interior file saved in PDF format, you're ready to upload them to CreateSpace.

First of all, you'll need to create an account with CreateSpace, which is easy enough and doesn't take long.

Once you've got that set up, log in and go to your "Member Dashboard."

From there, you can click on "Add New Title."

The next page CreateSpace will open has the headline, "Start your new project."

On this page, you'll provide three pieces of information:

1. "Tell us the name of your project."

2. "Choose which type of project you want to start" (where you'll choose "Paperback" from their list of options).

3. Choose a setup process

The last one gives you two options: "Guided" and "Expert."

Unless you're very familiar with this process, the better option is "Guided" – which provides help along the way. "Expert" is more streamlined and designed for those who already know the process and want to speed things up a bit.

After you're done with this page, and you hit "Guided," you'll land on a different page with the headline, "Title information." This is where you provide the metadata for your book:

1. title

2. subtitle

3. name of primary author

4. names and roles of other contributors (

5. whether the book is part of a series

6. the series title and volume number (if applicable)

7. edition number (whether it's the original version or an update, eg. "second edition")

8. language

9. publication date (which is optional; CreateSpace will automatically assign a publication date – the date on which you approve your book for publication – if you leave this blank)

Next is the ISBN page, where you'll tell CreateSpace whether you want them to assign you a free ISBN number, or whether you already have an ISBN number and want it connected with your new book, or whether you want a "custom universal ISBN," which costs $99.

I always go with the free ISBN option, which is the first.

Once you click on "Assign Free ISBN," CreateSpace will take you to a page with your new ISBN numbers, which cannot be changed.

Next comes the "Interior" page!

Here's where we decide on either "black & white "or "full color" and where we choose either white paper or cream. Cream paper is only an option if you choose "black & white." With full color printing, your paper color will be white.

You'll also choose your trim size, and CreateSpace will suggest 6" x 9", which is the most popular trim size and offers the widest distribution options. There are many other options available for trim size, but for nonfiction books, I prefer 6" x 9".

At this point, CreateSpace even offers a downloadable Word template for your interior, so if you're setting up your book before creating your interior (which is entirely possible), you could now download the interior template you need, based on your trim size.

Then you choose how you'd like to submit your interior.

Your choices are to upload your own interior file or to let CreateSpace design your book's interior (for a price – starting at $199). I think we're in agreement that the first option is the one we want.

Why should professional designers have all the fun?

Uploading the interior file

CreateSpace accepts the following formats for your book's interior: PDF, DOC and DOCX (Microsoft Word), and RTF.

If you're ready, select "Upload your book file" and click on "Browse" to find your interior file on your computer. Select it and CreateSpace will ask you to choose your "bleed" setting, which refers to how images are positioned within your book. Do they run off (end after) the edge of the page, or do they end before the edge of the page?

All the images I use within this book stop well within the margins, so I always choose "Ends before the edge of the page," which is pre-selected, anyway.

Next, you can scroll down and click "Save" to begin the upload of your interior file.

CreateSpace will then process your file and let you know whether it found any issues. You'll then get a chance to take a look at these issues by clicking on "Launch Interior Reviewer," which shows you how your interior file looks as a book and points out any issues CreateSpace found in the "Manuscript Issues" bar on the right-hand side.

If you need to make changes to your file, click "Go back and make changes." Otherwise, if everything looks fine to you, click "Ignore issues and save" to exit the reviewer and continue with the process of creating your book.

Uploading your book's cover

After this, CreateSpace will present you with options regarding your book's cover.

1. Build your cover online using CreateSpace's own "Cover Creator"

2. Pay for professional cover design (working with CreateSpace's expert team of designers), the price of which starts at $149.

3. Upload a print-ready PDF cover

If you've got your "print PDF" cover (designed with Canva), this is the time to upload it. Choose the third option, and click "Browse" to find and select your cover PDF file.

Once you see the name of your cover file in the upload window, you can "Save and Continue."

You should now see on the left-hand side of your CreateSpace page that "Interior" and "Cover" both have green check marks next to them. If they don't, go ahead and click on the one that doesn't and find out what CreateSpace still needs you to do.

Otherwise, look over the page with the ISBN numbers and the names of your interior and cover files, and then click "Submit Files for Review."

Review

CreateSpace will then complete the review of your files within 24 to 48 hours. I've usually found that they take closer to 24 hours, but I suppose it depends on the size of the book and any features that might require more time and attention.

When you see that green check mark next to "Complete Setup," you know that you've done everything you need to do for now, and all that remains is for you to wait until CreateSpace lets you know whether or not your book is good to go.

CreateSpace will email you to let you know when they've approved your files for publication. Then, it's time to take a look at your digital proof – by launching their digital proofer – to check and make sure everything looks good to you.

You can also order a paperback proof at this point, which I always like to do. You can either wait until you get a chance to look over the printed proof before you approve the file for publication, or you can approve the digital proof and let CreateSpace publish your book.

To wait or not to wait

I waited on the printed proof for my first book, **The Hypothyroid Writer**, but for the first journal I made, I approved the digital proof – shortly after ordering a printed proof to look over. I was anxious to get it published, but when the printed proof showed up, I found a formatting issue that didn't show with the digital proof.

That's when I went and fixed the interior file by making the left-hand outside margin a tick larger.

The interior file for my first book had been professionally formatted, and after scanning the interior file, I ordered a printed proof and found a formatting issue that my formatter fixed for me. I then uploaded the corrected file and, after review, approved it for publication.

It's up to you whether you'd rather wait on the printed proof, but I've found that to be a good bet. With the first I waited. With the second (my first journal), I didn't, and I ended up regretting that. It was easy to fix, and fortunately no one ordered a copy until after I published the corrected interior file.

Published!

Once you hit the "Approve" button, CreateSpace will invite you to make your book available to as many of its available sales channels as possible. Once your book is officially published and ready to order, you can order a final copy for yourself from the CreateSpace bookstore. If you've decided to make your book available on Amazon, it can take 3 to 5 days before its listing is live and ready for customers. With each of my own journals, though, it took less than three days' time before I could see the journal up for sale on Amazon and link it to my Amazon author page.

If you've made it this far, though, you're now a published author of a journal or workbook, which you can now either sell or give as gifts — or both.

In the next chapter, we'll go over what you can do next to market or share your new journal or workbook.

Making changes after your book is published

It's not unusual for authors to want to make changes to their books even after they're live on Amazon.

This is probably why KDP (Kindle Direct Publishing) and CreateSpace both make it so easy to do.

All you really need to do with CreateSpace is to go to your Member Dashboard and then select the book you want to change to get to its "Project Homepage."

From there, you can select "Interior" and click on the "Change" button to upload a revised interior file.

CreateSpace will warn you about what you can and cannot change (the ISBN and your book's trim size are locked and cannot be changed). After clicking through the warning, you'll get to "Choose how you'd like to submit your interior."

Under "Interior File," you can click on "Upload a different file" (beneath the name of the file already uploaded) and search your computer for the new interior file, select it, and hit "Save."

CreateSpace walks you through the process, and as long as you get to the see all green checks on the left-hand side of the screen – from "Title Information" to "Complete Setup" – you're good to go.

I went ahead and followed the steps I'm describing in this chapter, though I didn't actually upload a revised interior file. After clicking on "Save," I had the chance to preview the interior, and I can confirm that the shading of the text and lines I copied and pasted from Canva are visible in the previewer.

I think I assumed, at first viewing, that it wouldn't be visible in the printed copy. I was wrong.

So, as soon as I finish a cleaned-up copy of my interior, I'll go through this same process to upload it, preview it, and then – after looking over the digital proof – approve it for publication.

You can also change the cover, if you decide to make some changes to it in Canva – or to change it completely – by going through the same process but choosing "Cover" on your book's "Product Homepage."

One final note: you can either upload new files for the interior and the cover before hitting "Submit files for review, "or you can upload one or the other. But once you hit "Submit...," you can't go back and change anything else until CreateSpace is done reviewing whatever file or files you've just submitted.

So, if you've uploaded a new interior file and then submitted that for review, CreateSpace won't let you change the cover until it has reviewed the file you already submitted (for the interior).

Just something to keep in mind. Otherwise, this is a fairly quick and painless process.

If only keeping the house clean were this easy.

7

Your book is published! What to do, now?

I f the title of this chapter just made you smile (at least inwardly), then let me congratulate you for creating your first journal or workbook (or planner) using Canva and CreateSpace.

Now that you have a published paperback that will, at the very least, make a great gift idea or learning resource, what can you do now?

That depends on what your goals are – for your book and for your writing in general.

Do you want to make more journals or workbooks like the one you just created and published?

Or would you like to publish the same journal (if you've made a journal) with different cover design choices?

Maybe you'd like to take what you've learned and apply it to your first nonfiction book, novel, or collection of essays or short stories – to save yourself some money with the cover and to prepare and publish the paperback version of your book yourself, using CreateSpace.

Maybe all you wanted to do was to create some journals to give as gifts this year, and you're planning to wait on the reactions of those who receive them before you decide whether to make any more.

Whatever you're wanting to do with your book – or with future books – here are some things you can do to spread the word and give other people a chance to share in your excitement and to peek at your newest creation.

1. Share a link to your new journal on the CreateSpace store – along with an image of the cover – on Facebook and/or Twitter. Pinterest is another possibility, if that's one of your favorite social media sites.

2. Once the book is live in the Amazon store, make sure your book description is compelling – selling the benefits of your new journal and workbook and encouraging visitors to nab their own copies.

3. Create an Amazon author page for yourself, and link it to your journal or workbook (once it's live on Amazon). An author bio and picture helps put a human face on your new creation, and people are more likely to buy it if they like what they see on your author page. Put some thought into your author bio and choose a picture of yourself (or a drawing / self-portrait) that communicates warmth, along with other qualities you want book browsers to see. It doesn't have to be a professional photo (I refer to mine as my lunch lady selfie, since I'm wearing my "Monday" black polo shirt), but if you have one that you like, by all means upload it to your Amazon author page. Let people see who you are and why your project is important to you.

4. Join the Amazon Associates program, so that, once your book is live on Amazon, you can share affiliate links (complete with images) on Facebook and Twitter, which – if they lead to a sale – will net you not only your royalty but also some affiliate income with Amazon.

5. You can also use affiliate links to your books on your blog or website – using the "text" link (from your Amazon Associates banner), to create a hyperlink in the body of your blog post. Or you can post an

ad using the "text and image" option, by copying the code and pasting it into a text widget.

6. You can create a printed postcard/bookmark (designing a graphic for it on Canva and uploading it to VistaPrint or another printer of bookmarks, business cards, etc.) and offer it as a free gift to those who buy your book. All they have to do is contact you by email and attach a copy of their Amazon or CreateSpace order, and you'll write a brief, personalized note on the postcard, slap a stamp on it, and send it off to your customer's address (which they'd also have to give you, in exchange for your promise that you won't send them anything else or share their address with anyone else).

7. Or you can create that postcard and send it out to anyone you know who might be interested in the journal or workbook and letting them know how they can check it out (Search book name on Amazon, etc.).

8. You could also, of course, send out emails with the same information and with an attached graphic (created on Canva) that shows your journal's/workbook's cover and a compelling (and brief) description highlighting the benefits of the book you created. I usually prefer to go this route, because it doesn't cost me anything (other than time). But there's something about getting an attractive postcard in the mail from someone you know – and particularly about something they think you might like.

9. You could design a mug with an image of your book and use it where others will see it and (hopefully) ask you about it. Plus, you'll have a great new mug, and a constant reminder that you created something that millions of people could benefit from using. Vista Print makes mugs, too.

10. You could get a t-shirt made, too, with either an image of your book or some interesting, text from your journal or workbook (or planner). Even better if it's funny or at least thought-provoking. It could appeal to a powerful need – like the need (that many of us have) to get more important things done or to get work done more efficiently so we can spend more time with people we love – or to finally get that first novel written and published).

While with paperback books you can't take advantage of ebook promotions (unless you create an ebook version, which you can do with some workbooks), you can still do something every day to get the word out – on social media, on your blog (if you have one), or by showing a printed copy of your new journal or workbook to others.

Share other people's work, too, knowing (as you do) how hard it can be to market your own books and how much easier it is to market someone else's.

You could bring a copy of your journal or workbook with you and let people who know you see you using it yourself, but I don't know how many opportunities you'll have for doing this, and it may just be easier and more effective to show people the book and say, "Hey, look what I made!"

And when they ask you, "How did you make that?" you can tell them all about a nifty little book you bought on Amazon that made it so freaking easy, you just had to try, and boy, you're so glad you did!

But never mind that, for now.

I brought a paperback proof copy of my first book to work and had my fellow lunch ladies – who supported me all the way – sign it for me. My employer found out about my book from my supervisor and included my book in the company newsletter and advertised it at a company luncheon.

Everything helps.

Some things are more fun than others.

But if you want to sell more books, you'll need to either budget some time for book marketing or pay someone else to do it for you.

We make time for the stuff that's most important to us and that we enjoy doing – and we delegate or eliminate the rest. Or at least we become a master at neglecting it (hello, floor in need of vacuuming).

You might think that as a writer I'd rather write freelance articles than work as a lunch lady, but you'd be wrong. I've written – and ghost-written – freelance articles, and while I love writing, I do not love freelancing.

Truth be told, I'd rather spend my writing time writing books or connecting with others on Facebook and Twitter. I don't want writing to be associated with drudgery.

Writing books and designing covers for them are two of my favorite things.

Blogging is not. At least not blogging as part of a writing business.

And freelance writing gives me nightmares.

I enjoy the writing part – just not the stress of trying to write a value-packed blog post every week and making more people aware of each one as I publish it, because a blog no one knows about is unlikely to earn enough money to justify the annual cost of web-hosting and the plugins I've paid for to keep the blog secure and to back it up regularly.

Nor do I relish the stress of wondering if, after all the time I've spent researching and writing an article, my client will tell me it's just not quite what he had in mind.

Given a choice between ghost-writing articles and working as a lunch lady, I'll usually pick the latter. When I include the time spent researching before writing those articles, the pay per hour tends to be better with my lunch lady job, and it's a lot more fun.

Plus, it gets me out of the house, gives me a workout, and forces me to socialize.

Trust me when I say that socialization (meaning face-to-face interaction with other humans) might not happen otherwise. Ditto with exercise (other than my morning wake-up-workout, which is all of 20 push-ups and 20 squats, 'cause that's how long it takes for my first cup of coffee to heat up in the microwave).

So, for this year – or the next, if it's just around the corner – I hope you create something you'll be proud of, and I hope you cut something out that is cramping your style.

I'm cutting out weekly blogging (though I'm not ditching my blogs yet).

And I'm writing more books.

So, what are you going to create next? And how will it make your year better?

Conclusion

I hope you've enjoyed reading and using this book as much as I've enjoyed making it for you. I had such a ball creating my own journals —not to mention my own nonfiction books — that I had to share what I've learned about creating them using Canva and CreateSpace.

Researching the other journal and workbook offerings on Amazon and Barnes & Noble can help you decide how you want your cover to look and what features you want your book's interior to have.

I even bought a few to use myself.

What do you want your customers to get out of your journal or workbook? What would *you* want to get out of them?

This is important both before you create your first book and afterward. When you put something out there for others to see – and hopefully to buy and use – you learn more about self-publishing, and you can apply those lessons to your next books.

Sharing your experiences with others is also a great way to promote your book without pushing people to buy it (i.e., without being salesy). Share your mistakes and frustrations, as well as your triumphs, and others will love you for it.

Don't be afraid to be vulnerable as well as relentlessly helpful. Laugh at yourself and share what you've learned and what you'd like to do next.

And keep in mind what you like to read in other people's social media shares. It's not all about the book. It's about what you can do for your customer to help them to solve a problem or to thrive, and that goes beyond anything you publish.

Now that you've finished...

I would love it if you'd revisit this book's Amazon page and leave a review. You'll do me a huge favor, and you'll also be helping fellow book browsers who land on the page and wonder if the book can help them – as I hope it helped you.

I'd also love it if you'd connect with me on Facebook (lentzsarah) or on Twitter (@Write_It_Anyway) – or both. I'm also on Pinterest (SarahLentz95) and LinkedIn (lentzsarah), but I spend more of my social media time on Facebook (#1) and Twitter (#2).

If you have any insights you'd like to share, leave me a note on my blog's contact page at HypothyroidWriter.com or email me at sarahlentz@hypothyroidwriter.com.

About the author

After finishing her first NaNoWriMo in 2015 (and the first draft of her first novel) -- and reading The Miracle Morning for Writers – Sarah Lentz decided it was time to do what she had to do to get her first nonfiction book written and self-published by the end of 2016. So, she joined Self-Publishing School and wrote *The Hypothyroid Writer*.

A native of Oregon (Mt. Angel area), she now works part-time as a lunch lady in Minnesota (providing a daily workout and forcing her to socialize) and spends much of her non-lunch-lady time writing books and designing book covers for them.

She also crochets and dreams of using some of her writing income to pay someone else to do the housekeeping. She's borderline domesticated with a dash of wanderlust and a love for minimalism -- or at least a flavor of it that suits her and her family (husband, four kids, and a messy but adorable guinea pig).

Bonus chapter 1

Alternatives to Word for your interior file

We didn't always have MS Word here at home, and when we didn't (mostly because we couldn't afford it), we used OpenOffice – which is a free office suite that provides many of the same tools available with Microsoft Word.

I downloaded it to my computer to see if I could do everything I needed to do with the downloadable Word template from CreateSpace – and to make sure I could still create an interior file that CreateSpace would accept.

Our library network provides members free access to Lynda.com, which has an extensive library of tutorials for various software packages (among other things). It's a great research tool, and I'm taking advantage of the free access, because the basic monthly package costs $20. And I'm cheap.

OpenOffice.us.com provides access to the first few tutorial videos, but to watch them all, you need to take advantage of the free trial of Lynda.com. I'd check with your library network to see if they provide free access to Lynda.com for their members.

While working with OpenOffice, I was particularly interested in a number of things that I wasn't sure I could do as well or as easily in OpenOffice as I could in Word.

1. Creating a Table of Contents

To create a Table of Contents in OpenOffice, you'll need your chapter titles to be in Heading 1 format and your subheadings in Heading 2 format (and sub-subheadings in Heading 3 format) – just as in Word.

Then, you'll go into the Insert menu, click on Indexes and Tables and select Indexes and Tables from the submenu.

From there, you'll see a setup window with a left side that gives you a preview of the structure of your table of contents, based on the inputs on the right side, which is where you'll indicate how many levels you want your table of contents to have (for example, two levels includes the chapter titles and subheadings; three levels would also include sub-subheadings).

I kept "Protected under manual changes" unchecked, so I could delete the title and keep the one I already had on that page (centered and in the same font I use for Chapter titles).

I also kept "Outline" checked under the "Create from..." section, because honestly I didn't know what to do with the other options, and creating it from the outline does pretty much what I want it to do.

There's one thing about OpenOffice's TOC setup that I haven't figured out yet, and that's how to create a TOC without page numbers.

When it comes to creating eBooks, this is important. I'm creating this book in Word, because I need a TOC that has hyperlinks and no page numbers. OpenOffice will create a TOC with hyperlinks, but I've yet to figure out how to eliminate the page numbers, without going line by line and deleting them all manually.

I've searched the help menu, and the tutorials have, so far, not touched on this.

It's a sticking point for me – when it comes to ebooks – but so far, it doesn't stop us from creating an interior file for a paperback journal or workbook.

2. Changing the margins and creating "mirror margins" for a paperback book

This is easy enough to do from the Format menu. Once you select "Page," you see all the settings for page setup, including margins. You'll want to select "mirror margins" to set up the document as a book with inside and outside margins (the inside one including the gutter).

Set the top, bottom, and inside margin at 0.75 inches and the outside margin at 0.5 inches.

Then, you'll tackle #3.

3. Changing the page size to 6" by 9" (or whatever size you want, within reason)

This is something else you'll do from the "Page" setup window. Click on the "page size" tab and change the default type field to "User," which allows you to enter custom measurements.

Here's where you'd enter 6 inches for the width and 9 inches for the height, if that's your chosen trim size.

4. Adding clipart (and the ease of doing so)

The Gallery icon on the standard menu is where you can find clipart to use in your book. It looks like a framed portrait and sits roughly in the middle of your standard toolbar.

Click the icon to open the gallery, and click it again to close it.

You can also find free images online and insert them using the steps in #5 (below).

5. Inserting images and hyperlinks.

Open the Insert menu, point at "Picture" (in the bottom third of the Insert menu), and select "From File." Browse and select your image, whether it's a .jpg, a .png, or a .bmp.

Then, once OpenOffice loads it onto your page, all you need to do is resize it and position it where you want it.

6. Embedding fonts before exporting/saving the document as a PDF

I've searched the OpenOffice help pages, and I've found nothing about embedding fonts, so I'm banking on CreateSpace doing what it did for me before I even knew I needed to embed the fonts.

CreateSpace – during the preview phase (with the Interior Previewer) let me know my fonts were not embedded, but it did that for me (awfully nice of them). So, I'm gonna upload an interior file created in OpenOffice (sans embedding) and hope it will do the same for that one.

7. Using "drop caps" at the beginning of each chapter.

This was a biggie for me, because I like drop caps for the first paragraph of each new chapter. I wondered what would happen to the drop caps I'd put into Word, and whether the shading that OpenOffice put around them would show up in the PDF.

Turns out, it didn't. The drop caps looked shaded in OpenOffice but clean on the PDF.

My other concern was figuring out how to add drop caps if I hadn't had them in before.

All I had to do, though, was go into the Format menu, select "Paragraph," and then click on the "Drop Caps" menu tab. From there, I put a checkmark in "Display drop caps," (making sure my cursor was where I wanted the drop cap to show up), and I made sure the number of characters was "1" and line-height ("Lines") was "3."

The shading is still there around the drop cap. It doesn't seem to matter whether it's original to OpenOffice or not. But once the document is exported as a PDF, the shading disappears.

8. Setting and modifying text styles

I like being able to easily select text and change it to Heading 1 or Heading 2 format, and I also love being able to change the font, size, and color of those styles for the entire document by selecting some text, right-clicking on the style, and choosing "Update <style> to match selection."

It's a time-saver. And I wondered if I could do the same with OpenOffice.

Selecting text in OpenOffice and changing the style is easy enough. If you look at your formatting toolbar (below the standard toolbar, as long as it's turned on), you'll see on the far left a window that tells you the current style of selected text.

So, if I select some random non-subheading text in the body of my chapter, it should say "Default" in that window. But I can click on the down arrow to the right of that window and select "Heading 1," and suddenly the selected text takes on the same font and font-size (and justification) of my other Heading 1 text (chapter titles, etc.).

If I wanted to change the font of only the "default" text – throughout the book – I can select a chunk of regular body text, change the font, go into the Format menu, and select "Styles and Formatting." From the small pop-up window that opens, I can see that the selected icon is "Paragraph Styles," and those styles are listed below.

As I run my cursor over the icons, OpenOffice gives me their names. So, if I click on "Page Styles," it'll show me a list of page styles, and "Default" will again be highlighted, because the page where I've selected text is a page with a "Default" page style (as opposed to "first page" style, for example).

The right-most icon is the "New Style from Selection" icon, and if I click on it, it'll give me a submenu that includes the word "Update style."

So far, so good.

Except, when I select "Update style" – even after changing the font of my selected text – OpenOffice does ...nothing.

This is what happened in an OpenOffice document that I'd formatted for CreateSpace (with mirror margins). When I opened the OpenOffice document I'd kept for the ebook version and tried the same thing, clicking on "Update style" *did* change the font for all the "default" text in the book.

It also, strangely enough, pasted a copy of every image I'd inserted into the book right onto the title page.

So, after deleting all those images, I went back to the Introduction, selected the same bit of text, changed the font back, clicked on "Update style," and OpenOffice once again changed all the default text to the font I'd switched back to.

And this time, I didn't find a pile of pictures on my title page. But it does make me wonder (why on earth would it do that?)

I did the same thing with one of my chapter titles, changing the font and clicking on "Update style," and OpenOffice changed the font of every bit of text with "Heading 1" style. Then, I switched it back again. No picture pile on my title page this time.

So, I'm mystified, but still glad that OpenOffice does allow you to change the font and size of a particular text style for the entire document. The process could be smoother, but it works.

9. Adventures in page numbering

It's taking me a lot longer to deal with this particular issue. In the OpenOffice tutorials on Lynda.com – in their one near-useless video on page numbering – it suggests changing the page styles and applying different page numbering to the different page styles (but it doesn't bother showing you how to do this).

If you click on the icon to the left of the style field (on the far left of the formatting toolbar), it takes you right to the "Styles and formatting" window, which is where you can see their short list of "Page styles."

There's no "front matter" style or "appendices" page style. There's a "front page" (singular) page style, though, and I thought, "What if I just apply that style to all the front matter pages?"

So, I did that. But OpenOffice didn't like what I was doing, and the designation didn't stick.

Then I tried "Index" for all the front matter pages (other than the real "first page," which is my title page), and that worked.

Well, it worked after I went into the Insert menu, went to "Footers," and turned off (unchecked) "Index" to remove footers from the Index pages.

Except, my first numbered page – the first page of my Introduction – began with page number 6.

So, I had to find a way to make the page numbering start fresh (with #1) from that page onward.

After looking up "page numbers" in the OpenOffice help pages, I did the following:

1. I put my cursor at the top of the page that I wanted to be page number 1.

2. I went to the "Format" menu and selected "Paragraph."

3. I went to the "Text flow" tab, clicked on "Insert" under "Breaks," and went over to the page number field further to the right, and entered a number 1.

4. I clicked OK and checked my page number for the first page of my Introduction, and, sure enough, it had switched from "6" to "1."

5. I breathed a sigh of relief. And then I wondered, how do I add Roman numeral page numbers to the front matter pages – or should I leave well enough alone?

Not being able to leave well enough alone – because, after all, you might want those Roman numeral pages for your own journal or workbook (or some other book down the road) – I went to my first Index page (the copyright page), and, hoping that the new page sequence for the Default pages (beginning with my Introduction) would stick, created a footer for the Index pages.

Then, I went into the footer, centered the position of the page number, and went back to the Insert menu, picked "Fields," and selected "Page Numbers."

Then, I double-clicked on the page number, which opened a window that allowed me to set the format for my page numbers, and I chose lower case Roman numerals.

The first page – my title page – still doesn't have a footer, and I prefer it that way, but beginning with the copyright page, I now have Roman numeral page numbers (beginning with "ii") up to the first page of the Introduction, which still starts with a number 1.

So, now I need to regenerate the Table of Contents to update the page numbering.

10. Exporting or saving the .ODT document as a PDF document (for uploading to CreateSpace)

This is one of the cooler things about OpenOffice, because it has a button for this right on the standard toolbar.

You'll find the icon beneath and between the "Format" and "Table" headings on the menu bar. It looks like a mini PDF file icon (at least it did for me, when I squinted hard enough).

Click on that, and OpenOffice will create a PDF file based on the .ODT file you've been working on. The first thing it does is save the new

PDF to the destination of your choice. Then you can open it and take a look to make sure it looks the way it should.

From there, it's on to CreateSpace!

This chapter isn't a comprehensive tutorial on how to create interior files using OpenOffice, and you may run into a problem that I haven't dealt with here. I've included everything I had to deal with to make a paperback copy of this book, and I learn anything more, I'll add it as soon as I can.

If you run into problems not mentioned in this book, please feel free to drop me a note on my blog at HypothyroidWriter.com or email me at sarahlentz@hypothyroidwriter.com. You can also message me on Facebook (lentzsarah). I'll do my best to help you sort it out.

Bonus chapter 2

Canva For Work & uploading (up to 10) new fonts to Canva

If you're reading this, you're probably curious about the paid version of Canva – Canva For Work (CFW) – and wondering why I pay for it when I won't pay a little less per month for Photoshop.

I mentioned my tendency to overwhelm – and I'm not ashamed to admit that I resist jumping into programs that take hours of tutorials in order to figure out what all the tools do. Photoshop's free trial wasn't long enough for me to get comfortable enough with the program to pay for it.

With Canva, I could do plenty with the free version, and I used it so much that when Canva asked if I'd like to try Canva For Work, I was game.

Here's what persuaded me to stick with CFW after the trial period ended:

1. I get to upload ten extra fonts – which I change from time to time to eliminate the ones I never use and add a few new ones that I like from Google Fonts or one of the font websites I list in Chapter 3. One of my signature fonts (Dancing Script Bold) isn't among Canva's standard font offerings, so if I went back to the free version, I wouldn't be able to use it anymore.

2. I get to set my default fonts for headings, subheadings, and body text, and these chosen fonts are listed on my "Your Brand" page.

3. The "Your Brand" page is where I keep my brand colors, logos I've designed for my blog, and the fonts I've set (see reason #2). Because all my brand colors show up every time I want to edit the colors in a project, I don't have to constantly look for (or memorize) the hex codes for my favorite colors. It's a time-saver.

4. "Magic Resize" lets me take anything I've just made and resize it to fit a different purpose (say, from Pinterest graphic to Twitter graphic or Kindle cover to Wattpad cover or Barnes&Noble's Nook ebook cover).

5. I can change the dimensions of anything I've made to my own custom dimensions, so if I forgot to include the bleed area in my cover template, I could go into the File menu, hit "Change dimensions," choose "Use custom dimensions," change pixels to inches, and enter the dimensions I need. Too easy. I wish this option were available with the free version, but for now, you can only do this in Canva For Work.

6. Canva recently uploaded thousands of new templates to Canva For Work to make designing easier for premium members. So, while I wish those new templates were available to those using the free version, also, it does make CFW all the more appealing to me. So, if I choose a particular type of template, Canva For Work will have some brand new layouts for me to browse for ideas or to borrow and modify with my own content.

Uploading new fonts

On the "Your brand" page, you'll see the default fonts for "Add heading," "Add subheading," and "Add a bit of body text" – which you can change to your own default fonts.

Below that, you'll be able to upload new fonts – up to ten – to add to your Canva font offerings.

Once you've saved the .tff files for your favorite fonts from Google Fonts or another online source of free fonts – to your desktop or to a folder that's easy for you to find – you can simply browse for each font, one by one, and upload it.

Canva will ask you whether you own the font or have the right to use it. If you've downloaded it from one of the sources I've listed in chapter 3 (among other sources available online), you're good to go, so you can select, "Yes. Upload away!"

And you'll have some new fonts to play with.

For now, Canva limits you to ten, but I'm hoping they'll change that at some point. I'll go into my added fonts, now and then, and delete the ones I never use. Then I'll add some new ones that I'd like to try. Canva provides quite a selection already, so I haven't had a problem with this. If I really want a particular font, it's just a matter of deleting one of the fonts I don't use or want nearly as much (or at all).

After this glimpse into the world of Canva For Work, you may want to give it a spin to see if it's right for you. Canva offers a free 30-day trial. After that, if you want to keep it, you can pay for a year up front (at $9.95 per month) or you can choose a monthly subscription for $12.95 per month.

I'm not completely anti-Photoshop, though, and if you try them both and find that you'd rather pay $9.99 per month for the Creative Cloud Photography package – which includes "Photoshop, Lightroom, and more," there's a Journal Design Basics class I link to in the Resource pages at the back of the book that provides both Photoshop and InDesign tutorials.

What I most want to do with this book is help you create a journal or workbook (or planner) that you can be proud of, and I'd like to prepare you to continue creating beautiful and useful books for yourself and others.

If you find that Photoshop suits you more than Canva, I won't think any less of you. I'd rather you picked a program that you really enjoy working with (often).

There's nothing at all wrong with the program (as far as I know as an outsider). I wrote this book to help others like myself who have a greater tendency to overwhelm and who prefer a more ADHD-friendly interface, which Canva provides.

Ultimately, though, the program that works best for you is the one you'll enjoy using again and again.

Canva is that program for me, and I hope – after reading this book and creating your own journal and workbook using Canva and CreateSpace – you feel inspired to create more and to enjoy the process more and more.

After creating my journals, I felt more confident of my ability to learn more about book cover design and about formatting text for Kindle books and paperbacks.

I'm not an expert at any of it, but budget constraints have made versatility a must, and having created a journal of my own from start to finish has made me braver about tackling new and more challenging book projects.

I hope this book and your own creations do the same for you.

Resource List

Helpful articles on CreateSpace:

1. "Self-published Authors: Don't Make These 5 Newbie Layout Mistakes" – by Joel Friedlander (https://www.thebookdesigner.com/).

2. "9 Book Design Tips that Authors Need to Know" – also by Joel Friedlander

3. "Understanding Book Elements: Trim Size" – by Shawn, CreateSpace Graphic Arts Specialist

4. "Understanding Book Elements: Paper Color" – also by Shawn, CreateSpace Graphic Arts Specialist

5. File Uploading Tutorial (video) by CreateSpace videos (on YouTube)

6. "A Step-by-Step Guide to Formatting Your Book's Interior" by Kelly of CreateSpace Press

7. "Authors, Front and Center: How to Organize Your Front Matter" by Joel Friedlander

8. "Your Book's Back Matter: What You Need to Know" by Joel Friedlander

9. List of CreateSpace articles: "Formatting Your Files"

10. "Embedding Fonts in Your Document" by CreateSpace Resources

Books about Canva & designing books or book covers

1. *Ready, Set, Brand! The Canva For Work Quickstart Guide* by Lisa Larson-Kelley

2. *CreateSpace and Kindle Self-Publishing Masterclass – Second Edition: The Step-by-Step Author's Guide to Writing, Publishing, and Marketing Your Books on Amazon* by Rick Smith

3. *How to Make an Ebook Cover: For Non-Designers* by Kate Harper

Programs & courses for designing books or book covers

1. Journal Design Basics course with Kristen Joy Laidig

While I disagree about whether Photoshop is essential to anyone who's serious about creating professional-quality journals and workbooks, I enjoy this journal-making course, and it does provide tutorials on Photoshop and InDesign for those interested in broadening their design skill base.

Helpful Facebook groups

1. Self-Publishing Book Cover Critique & Help Group

2. Authority Self-Publishing

3. Canva's Inner Circle

Journals to check out (or even buy) to get ideas for your own journals:

1. *The Ultimate Idea Tracking Journal for Writers* – by Kristen Joy (pre-Laidig)

2. *The Busy Author's Book Marketing Journal: A 30-Day Journal to Help You Track Your Activity and Results* – by D'vorah Lansky

3. Sheri Farley's journals on Amazon (basic but in five different types to suit different journaling styles).

Workbooks to check out (or even buy) to get ideas for your own workbooks:

1. *Outlining Your Novel Workbook: Step-by-Step Exercises for Planning Your Best Book* by K. M. Weiland

2. *The Author Planner – A Workbook to Organize Your Writing Career: A Calendar Based Planner for Writers* by Sherrie McCarthy

3. *The Psychology Workbook for Writers: Tools for Creating Realistic Characters and Conflict in Fiction* by Darian Smith

Made in the USA
San Bernardino, CA
15 December 2016